All Things
Bright and Beautiful

To Tapishi

From your friend
& sister in christ
Diane

ALL THINGS BRIGHT
AND BEAUTIFUL

Paintings and Text by Laura Lewis Lanier

The C.R. Gibson Company · Norwalk, Connecticut 06856

Foreword
by
Leighton Ford

There is one God. And the one God speaks with one voice — in His word, the Bible, and in His world, His creation.

In this lovely little book, Laura Lewis Lanier has set forth in paintings and in words of inspiration how God discloses His truth, His beauty and His goodness. The combination is deeply moving and inspiring.

To many people, beauty is only a subjective reaction or an aesthetic judgment. But the Bible also speaks of the "beauty of holiness" — the beauty which is in God Himself and which He reproduces through His people.

Holy beauty does not come without pain. As the great saint, Augustine, said, "God had one Son without sin, He has no sons without suffering." Suffering and pain are often the tools that God uses to etch deeper beauty into our lives.

Laura Lewis Lanier has captured the truth of that beauty in *All Things Bright and Beautiful*. I am thankful for the gift that God has given to her and that she shares with us.

Introduction

As I paint and study landscapes and plants, I see the perfect order of creation in which God has so beautifully demonstrated His care for all of nature. One of my favorite Scripture verses, Matthew 6:30, perfectly illustrates the purpose in creating this book. *Jesus says, "And if God cares so wonderfully for flowers that are here today and gone tomorrow, won't He more surely care for you?"*

Many people today are struggling to survive. Sometimes we need to refresh our faith in God's providence with the beauty of God's word and God's world. Nothing is more powerful and universal for meeting our needs than the Word of God and the great hymns of faith and praise based on that Word.

Just as there are seasons in nature, there are cyclical patterns of change in our lives…each having its own purpose. Even though all of life is change, God never changes. His faithfulness, mercy and love are evidenced in all the seasons of our lives. God grants us strength for each new day while providing the assurance that all of our tomorrows are filled with hope and security. Nature itself is a bold witness to the steadfast care of His hand. We can compare God's seasons with the seasons of our lives.

A Time of Hope... a chance to begin anew. As we plant seeds based on these promises of God's word, we know a time of beauty and bounty is inevitable.

A Time of Faith... encouragement and promises of provision for our needs as we grow in the rich soil of God's word.

A Time of Harvest... the riches of His blessings are our inheritance as we harvest crops grown in the Master's field.

A Time of Surrender... experiencing growth and maturity as a result of circumstances we would not choose. God promises victory through darkness and songs in the night.

In everyday events, as well as the unexpected tough times, God's continuous guidance is always present to those who allow Him to be the Lord of their lives. That is, not choosing one's way, but rather asking, "What do You want for my life, Lord?"   These particular selections have been the strength of my life through joy and sorrow. As you read these powerful words of hope and encouragement from God's word, it is my prayer that you will come to know and trust in the One who made "all things bright and beautiful".

L.L.L.

A Time of Hope

As I've grown to know God and tried to put Him first in my life, hope has been something I could not strive for and attain, but I receive it as a gift from God.

Webster defines hope as *to desire with expectation of fulfillment; trust; to long for with expectation of obtainment, to expect with desire.* When our "hope is built on nothing less than Jesus' blood and righteousness," as one of my favorite old hymns states, the desire and expectation of this fulfillment can never disappoint us. It is only our own dreams, ideas, and plans that are outside God's desires for us that cause us to lose hope and be disappointed.

Hope and new beginnings are fresh every morning. It is not necessary to wait for a circumstance to bring hope. Hope, real hope, comes when we lay down our own ideas and plans...our mind, will and emotions... before God as a hand of cards dealt and say to Him, "How would YOU play them?"

L.L.L.

The Solid Rock

My hope is built on nothing less
Than Jesus' blood and righteousness;
I dare not trust the sweetest frame,
But wholly lean on Jesus' name.

When darkness seems to hide his face
I rest on his unchanging grace;
In every high and stormy gale,
My anchor holds within the veil.

His oath, his covenant, his blood
Support me in the whelming flood;
When all around my soul gives way,
He then is all my hope and stay.

When he shall come with trumpet sound,
Oh, may I then in him be found;
Dressed in his righteousness alone,
Faultless to stand before the throne.

On Christ, the solid Rock, I stand;
All other ground is sinking sand,
All other ground is sinking sand.

Edward Mote, 1832

He who believes in Him, who adheres to, trusts in,
and relies on Him, shall never be disappointed or put to shame.

1 Peter 2:6
The Amplified Bible

For the Lord is always good. He is always loving
and kind, and His faithfulness goes on and on to
each succeeding generation.

Psalms 100:5

*Jesus Christ the Son of God...
He isn't one to say "yes" when
He means "no." He always does
exactly what he says. He carries
out and fulfills all of God's
promises, no matter how many
of them there are.*

2 Corinthians 1:19-20

*If you abide in Me, and
My words abide in you,
you will ask what you desire,
and it shall be done for you.*

John 15:7
New King James Version

*Whatever is good and perfect comes to us from God,
the Creator of all light, and He shines forever
without change or shadow.*

James 1:17

*Never forget to be truthful and kind.
Hold these virtues tightly. Write them
deep within your heart. If you want
favor with both God and man, and a
reputation for good judgement and
common sense, then trust the Lord
completely; don't ever trust yourself.
In everything you do, put God first,
and He will direct you and crown
your efforts with success.*

Proverbs 3:3-6

*Happy is the man who has
the God of Jacob as his helper,
whose hope is in the Lord his God—
the God who made both earth and
heaven, the seas and everything in them.
He is the God who keeps every promise.*

Psalms 146:5-6

All Things Bright and Beautiful

All things bright and beautiful,
All creatures great and small,
All things wise and wonderful:
The Lord God made them all.

Each little flower that opens,
Each little bird that sings,
God made their glowing colors,
And made their tiny wings.

The purple headed mountains,
The river running by,
The sunset and the morning
That brightens up the sky.

The cold wind in the winter,
The pleasant summer sun,
The ripe fruits in the garden:
God made them every one.

God gave us eyes to see them,
And lips that we might tell
How great is God Almighty,
Who doeth all things well.

Cecil Francis Alexander, 1848

*Look at the lilies! They don't toil and spin,
and yet Solomon in all his glory was not robed
as well as they are. And if God provides clothing
for the flowers that are here today and gone
tomorrow, don't you suppose that He will
provide clothing for you? And don't worry
about food...what to eat and drink; don't worry
at all that God will provide it for you. All
mankind scratches for its daily bread, but your
heavenly Father knows your needs. He will
always give you all you need from day to day
if you will make the Kingdom of God your
primary concern. So don't be afraid, little
flock. For it gives your Father great
happiness to give you the Kingdom."*

Luke 12:27

Spring Prayer

Dear Lord,

Help me to lay down my own ideas and plans for my life, to be willing to trust You, and to accept Your plan for me. Show me how real hope comes through surrender to You rather than a fight for my rights. Give me a new beginning... a new life in Christ...so that I can forget what lies behind and reach forward to what lies ahead. Thank You that I can expect to receive the promises of Your word because You never fail.

L.L.L.

A Time of Faith

After walking several miles downhill on a hot clear day to get my last glimpse of a sunflower field near Cortona, Italy, I headed back up the hill knowing this was probably the last time of the season to photograph this mass of brilliant yellow faces looking intently toward the sun. It was as though they were an orchestra all tuned and ready for the conductor to begin this symphony of color bursting throughout the valley.

As I trudged back uphill on the long winding road leading "home," the heat seemed more intense than usual and the climb seemed longer and steeper than ever before. After a short while I came to a row of Italian cypress trees which lined the road in a rather even pattern. Their long conical structures cast great shadows providing what felt like a drastic change of temperature. I began to look forward to these places of refuge from the scorching sun, and the Lord brought to my mind a portion of Scripture I had known for years, although I had never given it special thought. In Psalm 121:5 we are told *The Lord is your keeper; the Lord is your shade on your right hand.* Suddenly, shade had an entirely new meaning to me! The Lord was demonstrating to me in such real terms how His power shades, keeps and protects the work of my hands. What a vast difference His shadow makes!

I believe, however, that what made this experience so very personal to me is the fact that it was the shade on my "right hand"...my painting hand! As long as I look to Him as my keeper, the Lord will provide what I need in my artwork as well as in other areas of my life. He protects and keeps all things that concern each of us who choose to be in His shadow.

L.L.L.

He Hideth My Soul

A wonderful Savior is Jesus my Lord,
A wonderful Savior to me:
He hideth my soul in the cleft of the rock,
where rivers of pleasure I see.

A wonderful Savior is Jesus my Lord,
He taketh my burden away;
He holdeth me up, and I shall not be moved,
He giveth me strength as my day.

With numberless blessings each moment he crowns,
To meet him in clouds of the sky,
His perfect salvation, his wonderful love
I'll shout with the millions on high.

He hideth my soul in the cleft of the rock
That shadows a dry, thirsty land;
He hideth my life in the depths of his love,
And covers me there with his hand,
And covers me there with his hand.

Fanny J. Crosby, 1890

What a God He is! How perfect in every way!
All His promises prove true. He is a shield
for everyone who hides behind Him.
He fills me with strength and protects me
wherever I go.

Psalms 18:30,33

No mere man has ever seen, heard,
or even imagined what wonderful things
God has for those who love the Lord.

1 Corinthians 2:9

God...He alone is my refuge, my place
of safety; He is my God and I am trusting Him.
For He rescues you from every trap, and protects
you from the fatal plague. He will shield you
with His wings! They will shelter you. His faithful
promises are your armor. Now you don't need to
be afraid of the dark any more, nor fear the dangers
of the day; nor dread the plagues of darkness,
nor disasters in the morning.

Psalms 91:1-6

"I tell you this—if two of you agree down here on earth
concerning anything you ask for, my Father in heaven will do
it for you. For where two or three gather together because
they are mine, I will be right there among them."

Matthew 18:19

Don't let others spoil your faith and joy with
their philosophies, their wrong and shallow
answers built on men's thoughts and ideas,
instead of on what Christ has said. For in Christ
there is all of God in a human body; so you have
everything when you have Christ.

Colossians 2:8-10

My God shall supply all your need according to His riches in glory by Christ Jesus.

Philippians 4:19
New King James Version

Don't be anxious about tomorrow. God will take care of your tomorrow too. Live one day at a time.

Matthew 6:34

Be strong and of good courage; do not be afraid nor be dismayed, for the Lord your God is with you wherever you go.

Joshua 1:9
New King James Version

This plan of mine is not what you would work out, neither are my thoughts the same as yours! For just as the heavens are higher than the earth, so are my ways higher than yours. As the rain and snow come down from heaven and stay upon the ground to water the earth, and cause the grain to grow and to produce seed for the farmer and bread for the hungry, so also is my Word. I send it out and it always produces fruit. It shall accomplish all I want it to, and prosper everywhere I send it. You will live in joy and peace. The mountains and hills, the trees of the field - all the world around you - will rejoice. Where once were thorns, fir trees will grow; where briars grew, the myrtle trees will sprout up. This miracle will make the Lord's name very great and be an everlasting sign of God's power and love.

Isaiah 55:8-13

Like A River Glorious

Like a river glorious
Is God's perfect peace.
Over all victorious
In its bright increase;
Perfect, yet it floweth
Fuller every day;
Perfect, yet it groweth
Deeper all the way.

Hidden in the hollow
Of his blessed hand,
Never foe can follow,
Never traitor stand;
Not a surge of worry,
Not a shade of care,
Not a blast of hurry
Touch the spirit there.

Every joy or trial
Falleth from above,
Traced upon our dial
By the Sun of Love;
We may trust him fully
All for us to do;
They who trust him wholly
Find him wholly true.

Stayed upon Jehovah.
Hearts are fully blest;
Finding, as he promised,
Perfect peace and rest.

Frances R. Havergal, 1874

Summer Prayer

Dear Lord,

Give me the confident assurance that what I'm trusting
You to do in my life is going to happen. Give me the
certainty that what I hope for is waiting for me even
though I cannot see it. Thank You for the blessings You
send every day to encourage me. Help me to look to You
for all my needs...for guidance and protection... because
You care about everything that goes on in my life.

L.L.L.

A Time of Harvest

A few years ago, a well-known author asked me to illustrate her book. I was elated with the prospect of seeing my work in print. However, I had learned that before I could commit to anything, I must seek God's will and counsel. As I sought His guidance, I felt much like a sixteen-year-old who had earned enough money to buy a car and whose Dad said *No.* God was definitely leading me against what sounded and looked like the chance of a lifetime for an artist. I did not understand what He had in store for me, and I could not see His plan at the time. With no real reason outside of trusting God, I declined the opportunity.

Shortly after I had said no, I was driving alone in my car one day when I felt God's presence. I did not hear an audible voice, but something spoke to me about creating a book that would use my watercolours with Scripture and my favorite hymns. Words can hardly express my thoughts and emotions of that day, but I knew this commission was from heaven and that through Him it would succeed.

God faithfully brought across my path every person I needed for advice and direction. *God provided all my needs according to His riches* and made a way for me to accomplish His purposes. Often one

cannot see or know except through the
eyes of faith that a certain thing will come
to pass. This book is a testimony to the fact
that when His seed is planted, it always
brings forth a harvest *in His time.*

L.L.L.

*We can make our plans, but the final outcome
is in God's hands. We can always "prove" that
we are right, but is the Lord convinced?
Commit your work to the Lord, then it will
succeed. The Lord has made everything for His
own purposes.*

Proverbs 16:1-4

When you draw close to God, God will draw close to you.

James 4:8

How Great Thou Art

O Lord my God! When I in awesome wonder
Consider all the worlds Thy hands have made,
I see the stars, I hear the rolling thunder,
Thy power throughout the universe displayed,

When through the woods and forest glades I wander
And hear the birds sing sweetly in the trees;
When I look down from lofty mountain grandeur
And hear the brook and feel the gentle breeze;

And when I think that God, His Son not sparing,
Sent Him to die, I scarce can take it in;
That on the cross, my burden gladly bearing,
He bled and died to take away my sin;

When Christ shall come with shout of acclamation
And take me home, what joy shall fill my heart!
Then I shall bow in humble adoration
And proclaim, my God, how great Thou art!

Then sings my soul, my Savior God to Thee;
How great Thou art, how great Thou art!
Then sings my soul, my Savior God to Thee;
How great Thou art, how great Thou Art!

Carl Boberg, 1886

Because the Lord is my Shepherd, I have everything I need!
He lets me rest in the meadow grass, and leads me beside
the quiet streams. He restores my failing health. He helps me do
what honors Him most.

Psalms 23:1-3

The eyes of the Lord search back and forth across the whole earth, looking for people whose hearts are perfect toward Him, so that He can show His great power in helping them.

2 Chronicles 16:9

I am the Vine; you are the branches.
Whoever lives in Me and I in him shall
produce a large crop of fruit.
For apart from Me you can't do a thing.

John 15:5

*For I am convinced that nothing can ever
separate us from His love. Death can't, and
life can't. The angels won't, and all the powers
of hell itself cannot keep God's love away.
Our fears for today, our worries about
tomorrow, or where we are... high above
the sky, or in the deepest ocean... nothing will
ever be able to separate us from the love of God
demonstrated by our Lord Jesus Christ when
He died for us.*

Romans 8:38-39

*Don't worry about anything; instead, pray
about everything; tell God your needs and don't
forget to thank Him for His answers. If you do
this you will experience God's peace, which is
far more wonderful than the human mind can
understand.
Fix your thoughts on what is true and good
and right. Think about the things that are pure
and lovely, and dwell on the fine, good things
in others. Think about all you can praise God
for and be glad about. Keep putting into
practice all you learned from me and saw me
doing, and the God of peace will be with you.*

Philippians 4:6-8

Oh, the joys of those who do not follow evil men's advice...scoffing at the things of God: but they delight in doing everything God wants them to do...thinking about ways to follow Him more closely. They are like trees along a river bank bearing luscious fruit each season without fail...and all they do shall prosper.

Psalms 1:1-3

For if you give, you will get! Your gift will return to you in full and overflowing measure, pressed down, shaken together to make room for more, and running over. Whatever measure you give—large or small—will be used to measure what is given back to you.

Luke 6:38

Autumn Prayer

Dear Lord,

Help me to see that we reap what we sow and that we will reap in due season if we do not quit trusting You. Teach me to sow seeds of faith based on Your promises rather than the temporary things of this world. Grant me patience to wait on You to bring the answer in perfection so that I may have Your best blessings. Thank You for making all things beautiful in Your time.

L.L.L.

A Time of Surrender

While spending time painting in the area of Italy known as Tuscany, I became accustomed to seeing grape vines growing on the hillsides. The older gnarled vines were beautiful to sketch because of their knotty twists and bends. Over the course of time, the winds, rains and sun - the weathering effects of the seasons - had forced their shapes. The most luscious growth came from these rugged old vines...grapes so heavy and bountiful they seemed to invite people to pick them.

In another vineyard were young plants which had suffered no ill effects of nature at all. They offered no particular beauty or character and were hardly worthy of my pencil or paintbrush.

As it is in nature, so it is in God's kingdom. From the winds and rains of adversity comes abundant growth and a beautiful life worth painting.

Do not be afraid to suffer. Do not be afraid to be touched with afflictions beyond your own ability to cope. It is from being shaken apart and not being destroyed

that one becomes strong and courageous.
By submitting to God through circumstances
beyond our control, we see the great depths
of His protection and provision.

   As we allow the tough times to
paint our lives, we become beautiful like the
gnarled grape vine and we bear luscious fruit.

L.L.L.

And now as you trusted Christ to save you,
trust Him too, for each day's problems;
live in vital union with Him.

Colossians 2:6

How Firm a Foundation

How firm a foundation, ye saints of the Lord,
is laid for your faith in his excellent word!
What more can he say than to you he hath said,
to you who for refuge to Jesus have fled?

Fear not, I am with thee, O be not dismayed,
for I am thy God and will still give the aid;
I'll strengthen and help thee, and cause thee to stand
upheld by my righteous, omnipotent hand.

When through the deep waters I call thee to go,
the rivers of woe shall not thee overflow;
For I will be with thee, thy troubles to bless,
and sanctify to thee thy deepest distress.

When through fiery trials thy pathways shall lie,
my grace, all sufficient, shall be thy supply;
The flame shall not hurt thee; I only design
thy dross to consume, and thy gold to refine.

The soul that on Jesus still leans for repose,
I will not, I will not desert to its foes;
That soul, though all hell should endeavor to shake,
I'll never, no, never, no, never forsake.

John Rippon, 1787

Jesus answered them,...
"These things I have spoken to you,
that in Me you may have peace.
In the world you will have tribulation;
but be of good cheer, I have overcome the world."

John 16:33

New King James Version

Jesus replied, ..."I will only reveal Myself to those who
love Me and obey Me....I am leaving you with a gift...peace
of mind and heart! And the peace I give isn't fragile like
the peace the world gives. So don't be troubled or afraid."

John 14:23,27

The Lord is near to the brokenhearted and saves
those who are crushed in spirit. Many are the afflictions
of the righteous; but the Lord delivers him out of them all.

Psalms 34:18-19

New American Standard

Great Is Thy Faithfulness

Great is thy faithfulness, O God my Father,
There is no shadow of turning with thee;
Thou changest not, thy compassions, they fail not;
As thou has been thou forever will be.

Summer and winter, springtime and harvest,
Sun, moon, and stars in their courses above
Join with all nature in manifold witness
To thy great faithfulness, mercy, and love.

Pardon for sin and a peace that endureth,
Thine own dear presence to cheer and to guide;
Strength for today and bright hope for tomorrow,
Blessings all mine, with ten thousand beside!

Great is thy faithfulness!
Great is thy faithfulness!
Morning by morning new mercies I see;
All I have needed thy hand hath provided;
Great is thy faithfulness, Lord, unto me!

Thomas O. Chisholm, 1923

Those who trust in the Lord for help
will find their strength renewed.
They will rise on wings like eagles; they will run
and not get weary; they will walk and not grow weak.

Isaiah 40:31

Good News Bible

The righteous cry and the Lord hears,
And delivers them out of all their troubles.

Psalms 34:17

New American Standard

Come to Me and I will give you rest -
all of you who work so hard beneath a heavy yoke.
Wear My yoke - for it fits perfectly - and let Me teach you;
for I am gentle and humble, and you shall find
rest for your souls; for I give you only
light burdens.

Matthew 11:28-30

For He, God, Himself has said, "I will not in any way
fail you nor give you up nor leave you without support.
I will not, I will not, I will not in any degree leave you
helpless nor forsake nor let you down (relax My hold
on you)!   Assuredly not!

Hebrews 13:5b
The Amplified Bible

If God is on our side, who can ever be against us?

Romans 8:31

Now glory be to God who by His mighty power
at work within us is able to do far more than
we would ever dare to ask or even dream of
- infinitely beyond our highest prayers, desires,
thoughts, or hopes.

Ephesians 3:20

Winter Prayer

Dear Lord,

Help me to be still, to cease striving, and to know that You are God...
that You are sovereign. Help me to see that my present sufferings
are not worthy to be compared with the glory that is mine in
Christ Jesus. Use this time to build Your character in me
as You teach me the lessons I need to learn. You know the beginning
to the end of this time of struggle and pain, and You will make a way
for me where there appears to be no way. Help me not to believe
everything I see and hear, but rather to trust wholly on Your Word
for guidance and to stand firm on Your promises.
What a comfort it is to know that You promise to meet all my needs.
Therefore I will cast away my anxiety and worries knowing
that nothing is too difficult for You, God.

L.L.L.

Designed by Bob Pantelone
Edited by Julie Mitchell
Type set in Palatino
Printed on Warren Patina Matte